CHESTER SOUTHAMPT
ORD READING SWIND
OCKPORT BIRMINGHAM
LEEDS SHEFFIELD W.
E NEWCASTLE CARD

OV
CHI
DG
RL
GC

IGHTON AND HOVE CHICHESTER SOUTHAMPTO
GOW CARLISLE NEWCASTLE CARDIFF EDINBU
ESTER OXFORD READING SWINDON LIVERPOO
KFORD SWINDON **PRESTON** LIVERPOOL CHICH
RLEY ELY LEEDS SHEFFIELD WAKEFIELD HUL
RGH GLASGOW CARLISLE NEWCASTLE CARDI
UTHAMPTON BRIGHTON AND HOVE CHICHEST
OOL MANCHESTER OXFORD READING SWINDG
OVENTRY CAMBRIDGE STOCKPORT BIRMINGHA
BEVERLEY ELY LEEDS SHEFFIELD WAKEFIEL
FF EDINBURGH CARLISLE NEWCASTLE GLASG
UTHAMPTON BRIGHTON AND HOVE CHICHEST
G SWINDON LIVERPOOL MANCHESTER OXFOF
RMINGHAM COVENTRY CAMBRIDGE STOCKPOF
S SHEFFIELD WAKEFIELD HULL BEVERLEY EL
RGH CARLISLE NEWCASTLE GLASGOW CARD
CHESTER SOUTHAMPTON BRIGHTON AND HOV
READING SWINDON LIVERPOOL MANCHESTE
OCKPORT BIRMINGHAM COVENTRY CAMBRIDG
LEEDS SHEFFIELD WAKEFIELD HULL BEVERL
E NEWCASTLE CARDIFF EDINBURGH GLASGO

PRESTON

WITH BLACKBURN, SOUTHPORT, MORECAMBE & CARNFORTH

Jane Brocket

yarnstorm
press

About the Brocket Pocket Guides This guide to Preston is part of a series of *Grand Provincial Tour Guides* and *Capital Tour Guides*, pocket-size publications which focus on the highlights and best aspects of provincial towns and cities in Britain, and areas of London. They consider the pleasures and details that make up the spirit and contemporary cultural life of a place: art, galleries, buildings, markets, colour, cafes, baking, books, flowers, and green spaces. The emphasis is on having a good afternoon or day out, seeing and doing things that are accessible to all, don't cost a fortune, and don't require advance booking.

Book your ticket and go. You will have a great time.

Jane Brocket grew up in Stockport, and was educated in Manchester, Bristol and Sheffield. She has been blogging since 2005 and is the author of fifteen books on a range of creative and cultural subjects. She lives in Berkshire with her husband, close to a train station with good connections. They have three children who live and study in London.

Also available by the same author
The Capital Tour Guide to Shoreditch

Forthcoming titles
The Grand Provincial Tour Guide to Coventry
The Grand Provincial Tour Guide to Oxford
The Grand Provincial Tour Guide to Norwich
The Capital Tour Guide to Soho and Fitzrovia

Contents

Introduction

There are two well-known reasons to visit Preston: the Harris Art Gallery and Preston Bus Station. The former is a nineteenth-century neo-classical temple to culture, and the latter is an iconic piece of Sixties Brutalist architecture, a masterpiece to some, a monstrosity to others. But there are more reasons to make the trip – they may be less obvious, but they are just as compelling: a superb, virtually unaltered 1930s café, a classic Victorian gin-palace pub, two spectacular public parks, a stylish arcade, many fine civic and domestic buildings, three secondhand bookshops, two markets, and all the pies, cakes and Lancashire specialities you could wish for.

Even though Preston was a boomtown during the Industrial Revolution, full of mills spinning and weaving cotton, it's a little different to the northern mill towns of popular imagination. It's far enough away from the once densely industrialised urban area of Manchester and close enough to the coast, the surrounding agricultural land and the Forest of Bowland in the north to feel embedded in the countryside (such lovely countryside, too). The wide River Ribble with its riverside walks is only a stone's throw from the city centre (Preston became a city in 2002) and open spaces are only ever a green hill or two away. As well as the setting, Preston has more of a Georgian legacy than you might expect in a place associated with cotton, and there is a modest and solid grandeur to the terraces in the older part of town below Fishergate, which were built with generous amounts of red brick on generously wide roads.

Of course, Preston has moved on since the heyday of famous local textile companies such as Horrocks and Courtaulds, and yet in some ways it has not changed much at all, and it is this sense of continuity and tradition that gives the city its special character. The textile industry may have gone, but this is a city with a true sense of place, one that has carried on going about its own business in much the same way as ever, not feeling the need to replace aspects of daily life with modern versions simply for the sake of it. Nor is this a dogged refusal to move on, because what has been retained is worth retaining, and the people of Preston are custodians of some fabulous traditions such as egg-rolling at Easter, holidays and fun fairs at Whitsuntide, tripe and trotters, and the Preston Guild which takes place every twenty years and is the last of its kind in the UK. Preston is a place to go to be reminded of the value of local and enduring tastes and habits.

Thanks to its geography, bus and train stations, and the fact that the Preston By-pass was the first section of motorway in Britain (it is now part of the M6), Preston is very well connected to many Lancashire and seaside towns. To make the most of its excellent location, this guide includes four of the most interesting places that can be easily reached from Preston. Blackburn is worth visiting for its sparkling cathedral, its charmingly old-fashioned art gallery and museum, and locally made sweets. Genteel Southport, where the tide – allegedly - never comes in, has the recently opened Atkinson with a lovely art collection, and the ever-stylish Lord Street. The Midland Hotel, a Modernist masterpiece, attracts visitors to Morecambe which has more besides: a sweeping bay with wonderful views, potted shrimps, second-hand books, and a classic café. Or take a train to Carnforth Station for a *Brief Encounter* moment in the restored Refreshment Room, and for one of the best bookshops in Lancashire.

This Grand Provincial Tour Guide tells you all you need to know to have an enjoyable and rewarding day of culture and civilized pleasures in Preston and surrounding towns. From art and books to architecture and parks, from good baking and coffee to markets and pies, it uncovers the very best in this part of the North West. Whether you are here for a couple of hours or a couple of days, with this Brocket in your pocket you will be able to make the most of your visit.

Getting there and arrival

Wherever you arrive from, the train journey to Preston is guaranteed to be full of interest and fine views. A trip up and down the line between Preston and Glasgow at any time of year is amazing thanks to the many dramatic changes in the incredible landscape, a day out from Manchester brings you through concentrated urban landscapes and former cotton towns before reaching the greenery of this part of Lancashire, and a journey from the south takes in the scenery of Staffordshire (highly underrated), and later there is Wigan and a glimpse of the Santus Toffee Works where they have been making Uncle Joe's Mint Balls since 1898.

As the train approaches from the south, there is the wide Ribble and its various bridges, the sloping, formal Avenham and Miller parks on the right, and then it's into the station (1880), grand and gloriously Victorian, with huge glass train sheds very jauntily done out in green, scarlet and white.

It's worth retelling the role the station played in the First World War because it's a good story. If you go the waiting room on platforms 3 and 4 you'll see a plaque commemorating the Preston Station Free Buffet that lasted day and night for four years in that very room. It was set up by a committee of Preston women and was funded by donations, and involved four hundred volunteers working twelve-hour shifts serving free hot drinks, biscuits and buns to a total of three and a quarter million servicemen, and it even had its own crockery (examples on display in the Harris Museum). It remained open through 1919 on reduced hours, and opened again in the Second World War when it served twelve million cups of tea. There were, apparently, many soldiers with fond memories of Preston station.

The exit brings you out on Fishergate, Preston's main street, and Brucciani's café (see page 42) is a couple of minutes away if you fancy some refreshments before going to the Harris Museum or the Bus Station (unless, of course, you arrive by bus).

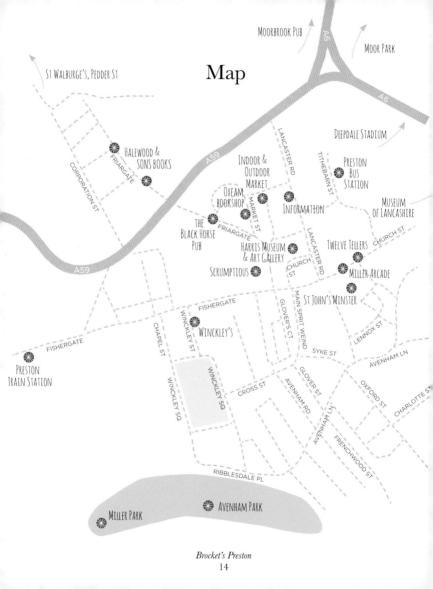

Map

Moorbrook Pub

Moor Park

St Walburge's, Pedder St

Deepdale Stadium

Halewood & Sons Books

Indoor & Outdoor Market

Preston Bus Station

Oxfam Bookshop

Information

Museum of Lancashire

The Black Horse Pub

Harris Museum & Art Gallery

Twelve Tellers

Scrumptious

Miller Arcade

St John's Minster

Fishergate

Winckley's

Preston Train Station

Winckley Sq

Miller Park

Avenham Park

Ribblesdale Pl

Corporation St

Friargate

Lancaster Rd

Tithebarn St

Market St

Friargate

Church St

Church St

Lancaster Rd

Chapel St

Winckley St

Glovers Ct

Main Sprit Weind

Lennox St

Syke St

Avenham Ln

Cross St

Avenham Rd

Glover St

Avenham Ln

Oxford St

Charlotte S

Frenchwood St

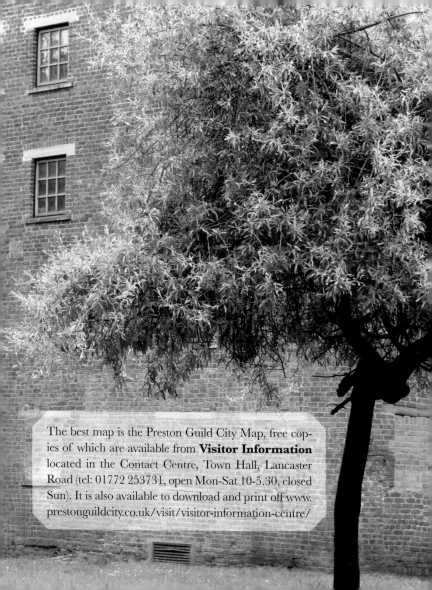

The best map is the Preston Guild City Map, free copies of which are available from **Visitor Information** located in the Contact Centre, Town Hall, Lancaster Road (tel: 01772 253731, open Mon-Sat 10-5.30, closed Sun). It is also available to download and print off www.prestonguildcity.co.uk/visit/visitor-information-centre/

Preston's
highlights

The Harris Museum & Art Gallery is worth visiting both for its collections and for the building itself. It is a remarkable edifice which houses one of the country's most impressive provincial galleries, a breathtakingly large Greek temple right in the middle of a mill town, and it dominates the large Flag Market in all the right ways. It was commissioned by the trustees of ER Harris who left part of his fortune to Preston and it contains, as he wished, a museum, an art gallery and a free library. The Harris was built 1882-93 by James Hibbert, a local architect, and this is his finest building, one which reflects the contemporary conviction that art and architecture should and could have an uplifting and improving effect (something the large inscriptions on the exterior make clear). With its height, gigantic portico and decorative pediment, this neo-classical building expresses immense Victorian confidence and conviction. Inside (and out) it is gloriously full of Greek and Egyptian references, patterns, friezes, palmettes and details (have a look at the stair balusters) which work together to create an incredibly rich interior. There is a central hall that rises through four levels and an 'Egyptian balcony' – it really is a matter of looking up and down all the time to take it all in. On a rather less elevated level, the radiators in the café area and main galleries are also worth noting; they are the massive, cast-iron, beautifully detailed, twelve-pipe originals which have been nicely conserved – no doubt they made the Harris a warm and welcoming place in the days before central heating was taken for granted.

Today, the Harris is a friendly, well-run, energetic and enterprising place. It plays to its strengths but always with an eye on the modern. Since its inception, it has had a policy of collecting and displaying new work and is in the fortunate position of having rooms large enough to show substantial exhibitions of contemporary art alongside the traditional and historical collections. (In collaboration with artist Nathaniel Mellors, the gallery was a recent winner of the prestigious Contemporary Art Society's Award for Museums.)

The permanent art collection is too little known, and is a secret that should be shared more widely. It has a fair amount of the Victorian portrait, genre, melodrama and landscape paintings you'd expect in a gallery established in the nineteenth century to improve and educate the locals, often by big names of the period (John William Waterhouse, William Etty, Richard Dadd and Arthur Hughes). But it really comes into its own with its holding of twentieth-century art. What you see depends on the current display, but there's a good chance you'll find paintings and sculpture by some very well-known artists in grand galleries with parquet floors, high ceilings, and lots of light and space. The Harris owns work by the likes of Stanley Spencer, Maggi Hambling, Dame Laura Knight, Frank Auerbach, Bridget Riley, Charles Ginner, LS Lowry, Ivon Hitchens, Cedric Morris, Carel Weight, and Jacob Epstein, but it also has some fine paintings by local and lesser known artists such as *Preston* (1953) by Charles Cundall, *Why War?* (1938) by Charles Spencelayh, and the extremely popular *Pauline in the Yellow Dress* (1944) by Sir James Gunn.

In addition to the fine arts, the Harris has some unusual and intriguing strengths including glass (drinking glasses and the Mrs Seddon Collec-

tion of English Coloured Glass) and the bequest of Mrs French who donated the largest scent bottle collection in the UK. There are display cases full of trade, calling, and cigarette cards and card holders, and a lovely collection of spectacles including 'quizzers', pince-nez and lorgnettes. There is a good deal of excellent pottery and porcelain, from special Preston Guild and Preston Temperance Society commemorative pieces, to Staffordshire china, to ordinary, everyday dining-room table sets. It's not terribly posh or priceless, but it's meaningful and very engaging.

The museum also has an outstanding textile and costume collection which includes many post-war, off-the-peg Horrockses dresses featuring gorgeously imaginative, cleverly designed, often highly floral cotton fabrics. There is a wonderful model of the huge Horrockses Yard Works complex in the Discover Preston room which works hard to fill the visitor in on important aspects of Preston's history including football, textile mills, Richard Arkwright, Samuel Horrocks, and the birth here of teetotalism. (Part of Horrockses' Centenary Mill (1891), now apartments, is still on New Hall Lane.)

Downstairs is the library, and a café warmed by the giant radiators where they sell Lancashire cheese sandwiches, Lancashire crisps and cakes and biscuits made by local bakeries (open 10-4). There is also a small bookshop with a very good selection of postcards of paintings.

Just outside in the square is the Cenotaph (1926) designed by Sir Giles Gilbert Scott which was recently - and beautifully - restored as part of the Preston Remembers project (www.prestonremembers.org.uk). The sculptural work was done by Henry Alfred Pegram and includes one of the many Preston lambs to be found around the city.

Finally, the toasted tea-cakes at Scrumptious, opposite the Harris at 36 Market Place, are highly recommended. They come piping hot and dripping with butter, and are undeniably delicious with a mug of strong tea.

i FREE, OPEN MON 11-5, TUES–SAT 10-5, CLOSED SUN AND BANK HOLIDAYS

▶ MARKET SQUARE (AKA FLAG MARKET) TEL 01772 258248

@ WWW.HARRISMUSEUM.ORG.UK

Preston Bus Station The debate about the Bus Station is a heated one. Is it an eyesore or a Brutalist beauty? Should it be knocked down or should it be preserved? After years of being at risk, it was granted Grade II listed status in 2013, but as listing can be a double-edged sword which prevents both development and destruction, the future for the building is not clear. Whatever your taste in architecture, though, it is worth seeing before it changes or goes. Nothing quite prepares you for its sheer vastness; it's enormous, the size of two football pitches, with enough spaces in the car park above for more than a thousand cars, and it has a claim to being the largest bus station in Europe, although it does beg the question why it was deemed necessary to have eighty bus stands in a relatively small town - now city - like Preston.

In fact, despite its air of melancholy, the coldness in winter, and the associations that all bus stations tend to accumulate (since when has any British bus station ever been a bright, warm, upbeat place?) it's a pretty incredible Sixties building, one of the most significant Brutalist buildings in Britain, hence all the hoo-ha. It remains largely as it was when it was built by Ove Arup and Partners in 1969 to a design by Keith Ingham

and Charles Wilson of the Business Design Partnership (but it's now not quite as white as some recent photos suggest). No matter where you stand on the question of aesthetics, the sheer length and majestic simplicity of the four curved concrete car park balconies are astonishing and there's bravura to the whole thing, which in a way mirrors the bravura of the Harris Museum. Inside, nearly all the original fixtures and fittings remain; there are signs in the then-new Helvetica typeface (and some dire modern ones), huge dual-design clocks (the once-revolutionary new digital clocks below the clocks with hands have now stopped), a roof made of concrete beams, and curvy wooden seating. It could all benefit from a measure of restorative cleaning and attention, not so much that the patina of age and use is destroyed, but just enough to maintain the authenticity that makes this a real, living, useful building rather than a preserved-in-aspic shrine to the Sixties.

Today, the Bus Station gets very mixed reviews, but there are many locals who do not want to see it demolished and there are many architectural historians, writers, and modern architecture enthusiasts who support it passionately. If it is given a new lease of life, the setting, surroundings and connections with the rest of the city need to be improved in order to make it more integrated and even more impressive.

TITHEBARN STREET TEL 01772 556618
WWW.PRESTONBUS.CO.UK

Indoor & Outdoor Covered Markets The joys of an authentic, local, week-in, week-out market cannot be overstated. While many other towns and villages in Europe have kept their traditional markets, in Britain we have let most of them disappear or fade to almost nothing, or be reduced to just another location for a group of travelling stalls. So it's a delight to come across a place with a real market which is full of personality, personalities, and good local produce.

Between Market Street and Lancaster Road is the covered outdoor market which has been here since the 1870s, and is a huge structure with an enormous high wooden roof held up by cast iron pillars. On one side of it is the smaller former fish market which was covered in 1924, and on the other is the more recently built indoor market with food stalls on the ground floor and non-food stalls and a café upstairs. Although the Covered Market is grand and impressive, and similar in style to the big old London markets, it's also under-used and very cold in winter, which means this historical, characterful area is under threat of closure.

So, too, is the indoor market in its dated but still very practical 1972 building. But whatever happens with the indoor market, it needs to be retained in some form as it is undoubtedly one of the best truly local markets in Britain. It's almost medieval in essence with fishmongers, butchers, pie-sellers, bakers, greengrocers, stalls selling butter, eggs and cheese, a confectioner, a florist or two, a tobacconist, and a café. Most food is seasonal and comes from local farms and suppliers, and there is no fussiness or squeamishness. A whole, fresh pig's head can be bought for £3, a pig's foot for 50p, and tripe and black pudding are still popular. There is wriggly, slippery stuff in the form of whelks, cockles, winkles and snails, and plenty of fresh fish from the coast. Other stalls sell hens' eggs, duck eggs, goose eggs, fresh butter, and many different Lancashire cheeses, some mild and creamy, some tangy and crumbly. The bakers

CLAYTON PARK
BUTTER
PIES
£1·00
EACH

SALTED
Butter
250g ℮

Greenfields
SALTED
Butter
250g ℮

Greenfields
SALTED
Butter
250g ℮

GREENFEILDS
BEST BUTTER

COCKLES
£2 PER 100g

COCKLES
IN VINEGAR
£2 PER 100g

WHELKS
£1·60 PER 100g

WHELKS
IN VINEGAR
£1·60 PER 100g

MUSSELS
£1·60 PER 100g

MUSSELS
IN VINEGAR
£1·60 PER 100g

RAYFISH
TAILS
£2 PER 100g

ROLL MO
70P EACH

FRESH PEA-PODS
£1·80 PER POUND
per sq.

FARM FRESH
DUCK EGGS
£1·80 1/2 DOZEN
£3·60 DOZEN
packers N° U·K·2·997
BEST BEFORE 21·6·14

LOCAL CAULI
99
EACH
class 1.
P

Fresh
Pigs Feet
50p each

Adrian Livesey
The Butcher Of Choice
f like us on Facebook

Fresh
Pigs Tails
29p each
or 4 for £1

Adrian Livesey
The Butcher Of Ch

HOME
MADE
CHORLEY CAKES
£
2 FOR 2·20

have barm cakes (soft, flat bread buns), pasties, steak puddings and pies, so many pies, including jellied pork pies, beef pies, butter pies, (filled with potato and onion), seasonal fruit pies, and big, wobbly custard tarts with nutmeg on top, vanilla slices (Lancashire's answer to the *mille-feuille*) and little-known Manchester tarts (pastry, jam, custard, coconut). Then there are the cakes which aren't really cakes at all; Eccles cakes (currants and puff pastry, all flaky and dense), Chorley cakes (currants and short-crust pastry, the thin plate-size ones are the best, and can be spread with butter), and potato cakes which are delicious toasted for breakfast or with a cup of tea. In fact, the range of cheap, tasty and filling foodstuffs here made with flour and pastry is quite staggering. If a juicy, fresh, crisp antidote is needed, go to the stall of Matt Wade, 'Banana King', who sells a huge range of fruit and veg (and 'parching' peas – see page 108 for recipe).

(Note: Greenhalgh's Bakery ('since 1957') on nearby Orchard Street and Fishergate sells another cake variant, the flat cake, which is a slightly thicker, more succulent Eccles cake. The other local Lancashire baker to look for is Williams.)

i INDOOR MARKET OPEN MON–SAT 8–5, MOST TRADERS OPEN 9–5

▶ OFF EARL STREET

@ WWW.PRESTON.GOV.UK/BUSINESSES/MARKETS/INDOOR-MARKET

i OUTDOOR COVERED MARKET OPEN MON, WEDS, FRI, SAT 9.30–3.30 (CAR BOOT AND FLEA MARKET TUES AND THURS)

▶ OFF MARKET STREET AND EARL STREET

@ WWW.PRESTON.GOV.UK/BUSINESSES/MARKETS/OUTDOOR-MARKETS

Miller Arcade It's a shame that there is not yet more going on in Preston's Miller Arcade, as it is clearly an ideal candidate for revival and reuse, and would be even more interesting if it were busy and filled with energetic, independent businesses. It's an absolute beauty, a grand old glass-and-tiles arcade built on a square plan with an entrance in the middle of each of the four sides. Unlike many arcades in places like Hull, Leeds and Cardiff which run between buildings and are almost hidden from view, this one stands unattached, proud and in great condition. Fortunately, there are at last signs that notice is being taken of this gem of a building.

It was built in 1899 in a decidedly grand, ornate but not too ornate, Paris Beaux-Arts style, a complete contrast to the mostly plain, solid, red brick Preston architecture (although there are more good retail facades on Fishergate – see page 52). Inside it's filled with light so that you can enjoy the clean and well-maintained decorative glazed tiling, the arched glass and iron roof, and the sense of retail elegance and glamour. The only negatives are the modern floor tiles, and the fact too many of the shops are empty.

At one time the arcade was a thriving home to many upmarket businesses including a hotel and even Turkish Baths, although why you'd want to mix shopping and steaming, I don't know. (The ornately lettered sign over the old Lancaster Road entrance to the baths is clearly visible). In an interesting cameo appearance in *A Kind of Loving* (1962) it forms a glittering, brightly-lit retail backdrop to the cinema scene with Alan Bates, but for many years it has looked forlorn and disconnected from the retail life of Preston despite the various businesses upstairs. Fortunately, though, things are now looking up for the Miller Arcade

with the recent arrival of the smart Olive Tree Brasserie which serves Greek dishes in a modern interior (www.olivetreebrasserie.co.uk, tel 01772 825888) and plans for more investment and renewal, including the possibility of converting the upper levels into apartments.

i GENERALLY OPEN MON-FRI 9-5, SUN 10-4

» CHURCH STREET

Avenham and Miller Parks Unless you knew about them, you wouldn't realise as you make your way down Fishergate that a few minutes' stroll away from the shops and crowds are two of the most interesting, beautiful, municipal Victorian parks in the north of England. Avenham and Miller parks are next to each other, separated by the old East Lancs Railway embankment and connected by a path under the railway bridge near the river. The land was given by local grandee, Henry Miller, and the parks were designed in the 1860s as an employment scheme when workers were laid off because of lack of cotton due to the American Civil War.

Once you walk southwards from Fishergate, you see that the land below it slopes down in a wide, curving, natural amphitheatre to the banks of the River Ribble. This has been used to create a huge expanse of green in the more informal Avenham (perfect for the annual Easter Monday egg-rolling event), and more formal clipped lawns in Miller. Both parks are lovely places to sit, run, roll, or walk - the tall lime trees that line the straight edge of the river bank create a particularly lovely path – or for a wander to see the Swiss Chalet, Belvedere (open-sided summer house), Boer War Memorial and large, nicely planted 1930s Rock Garden in

Avenham, and the very formal Italianate terrace with urns and statue of Earl of Derby, majestic fountain, neat flower beds and roses, and newly restored grotto in Miller. There are wonderful views beyond with the river, bridges, fields and lots of sky, and to the north is the grand, red, former Park Hotel (1882) which was the railway hotel and is now offices.

Curiously for a place with such fine Victorian credentials, this is also where you find Preston's most successful and innovative modern building, the Pavilion Café designed in 2008 by Ian McChesney. It sits at the bottom of the long slope in Avenham Park, fitting in perfectly with the setting of grass and water and trees. It is a mostly glass and timber building in a gently tapering crescent horn shape with a spiky, zig-zag cantilever roof, and tall windows that create a feeling of the outside coming in. The Pavilion has several rooms and is used for meetings, concerts, and performances and it also houses a very modern and spacious café with a Scandinavian feel which serves breakfasts, sandwiches, cakes, tea and its own blend of coffee (it's a nice place for a full English after a Preston parkrun (www.parkrun.org.uk) or a brisk walk by the river). The café is open 10-5 April-Sep, 10-4 Oct-March.

𝑖   OPEN DAILY

@   WWW.AVENHAMPARK.ORG

Books

Halewood & Sons After visiting so many towns and cities that are now without a single independent second-hand bookshop, it's wonderful to discover that that Preston has two, and that they are totally crammed with good books. They are owned by Halewood & Sons (established 1867), are very much part of Preston life, and still going strong. The two shops are on Friargate which, before the ring road (Ringway, A59) cut across it, would have had all the hallmarks of a great local high street (it still has a fine mix of façades). Now, though, it feels somewhat separated from the main, central shopping area, even though the shops, some of which have been here for years (such as Margaret Mason florist, at number 85 since 1961) are only a few minutes' walk from the Harris Museum and Art Gallery.

In the Halewood shop at number 37 the neatly arranged books fill the shop from floor to ceiling. Here they sell antiquarian books and are strong on sport, birds, railway, biography and local interest. It may look slightly serious, but you soon see that the selection is very eclectic and not at all intimidating. (Next door is the Grade II listed Old Black Bull pub, c1900, with a flamboyant exterior.)

The second Halewood & Sons shop is further up on the same side at number 68. From the outside there is little indication of what is going on inside, and the fact that it is completely and utterly full of books, full to bursting, full to the point where it's tricky for a customer to move around and positively reckless to go downstairs between the two tall stacks

that line the entire stairwell. So breathe in and be prepared to browse through the phenomenal range of books here. There is a good Sherlock Holmes section, and lots of Penguin paperbacks, but then it seems most categories are well represented in the wobbling towers of books.

i OPEN: MON–SAT 10.30–5 (THURS 10.30–4)

⏩ 31 FRIARGATE TEL 01772 252603 AND 68 FRIARGATE TEL 01772 252613

Oxfam A model Oxfam second-hand bookshop on the other side of the Flag Market to the Harris. It is intelligently laid out, well organised, and has very good stock. The fiction, drama, poetry, children's and foreign language sections are all strong, but there is also an excellent mix of mainstream, esoteric, older and collectible books.

i CONTACT SHOP FOR OPENING TIMES

⏩ 34 MARKET STREET TEL 01772 881590

@ WWW.OXFAM.ORG.UK

The Book Stop's Here The pun is intended at this large second-hand and discounted book stall on the outdoor market which is a long-established local business. It has a great number of books, an eye-catching way of displaying them on the tables, and is strong on popular paperback fiction and 'misery memoir'.

i OPEN MON, WEDS, FRI, SAT, CHECK TIMES ON FACEBOOK PAGE

⏩ OUTDOOR MARKET TEL 01772 713744

@ FACEBOOK 'THE BOOK STOP'S HERE, PRESTON MARKET'

Refreshments

Brucciani's Café If you have only a short time in Preston, then the café you really need to know about is Brucciani's. It's the most amazing period piece which, instead of kowtowing to fashion and repositioning itself as 'vintage', has simply carried on doing what it's been doing since 1932: serving unpretentious teas, coffees, cakes and refreshments in exceptional premises that have hardly altered since the Thirties. The exterior has beautiful curved plate-glass windows, a lovely square light advertising fresh cream and cigarettes, and the Brucciani name written with a flourish in large cursive lettering. Inside, it's like stepping into an old café in France or Portugal complete with dark colours, lots of gilt, mirrors, framed photos, old-fashioned café tables and chairs and, perhaps more in keeping with Preston, painted signs for prime sausages and Bovril and drinking chocolate. The pretty stained glass window at the back should be admired – in fact, everything in here should be. It's like a set (black and white photos make it look as though it's in a 1930s film) but it's all for real and is still very popular with locals of all ages. Service is fast and friendly and there's a good range of down-to-earth, affordable snacks and meals and, while it may have gone over to paninis, first cousin of cheese toasties, it still does a great cup of tea with a slice (currant, almond, Bakewell). It's very close to the station, but don't leave it too late to visit as it shuts pretty early (4.30pm or so).

i OPEN (APPROX.) MON–SAT 8–5, SUN 10–4

⟩ 91 FISHERGATE TEL 01772 252406

@ FACEBOOK PAGE 'BRUCCIANI'S PRESTON'

The Black Horse Pub Old pub interiors can be both beautiful and brilliantly atmospheric, especially if they date from the Victorian period when there was seemingly no limit on how many light fittings, mirrors, grand fireplaces, how much fancy tiling, etched glass, and wood panelling could be squeezed in to make a pub glitteringly bright, warm, cosy and alluring. The Black Horse is one of these, a cut above many other more down-to-earth pubs in Preston by dint of once being attached to a hotel and therefore wanting to impress. It was built in 1898 and very little has changed apart from the U-shaped seating area behind the bar which replaced a Market Room in 1929. There are still two little snugs with fireplaces (one with William Morris wallpaper), a lovely mosaic floor running through from the grand entrance with the pub's name spelt out in deep blue letters. In the main room, as well as a huge ceramic fireplace is the most amazing semi-circular ceramic bar topped with wood which is one of only eleven remaining ceramic counters in the country. Then there's lots of Arts & Crafts-influenced stained glass, some lovely etched glass, and huge amounts of dark red wood in the doors, panels and staircase which all add up to create an exceptional drinking venue. It's now a Robinson's pub (Robinson's is the well-known brewery in Stockport), but a tea or coffee is just as good if you want to sit and enjoy this amazing interior.

i OPEN MON-THURS 10.30AM-11PM, FRI-SAT 10AM-MIDNIGHT, SUN MIDDAY-10.30PM

🕨 166 FRIARGATE   TEL 01772 204855

@ WWW.BLACKHORSE-PRESTON.CO.UK

Parched Peas If they knew about it, Preston would have many food writers in raptures. Perhaps, though, it's just as well they don't, because the great thing about Preston's specialities is that they are still very much a feature of everyday life here, and not part of a modish rediscovery of a culinary heritage or a self-conscious resurrection of quaint ingredients and old recipes. The Flag Market in front of the Harris Museum is now used mostly for events, but this is the place to come for one of these specialities: parched peas. All year round there are a couple of stalls here selling little pots of hot, dark brown peas which are sprinkled with vinegar and eaten with a spoon. They are a Prestonian (and Lancastrian) speciality traditionally associated with fairgrounds (when they used to be served in white mugs – now replaced by white polystyrene cups) and Bonfire Night, and are quite different to fish and chip shop mushy green peas. They are made with parching peas which are soaked overnight and simmered slowly until cooked and beginning to burst. Although there is some liquid, they are firmer than mushy peas, with a deeper, earthier taste, and they are deliciously comforting, filling, and easy to make (there is a recipe on page 108).

i DAILY, ALL YEAR ROUND

▶ FLAG MARKET

Yates's Blobs Just as warming, especially if you've just come off the market or from the Bus Station in cold weather, is a Yates's blob (or 'hot blob'). Although Yates's is now a nationwide chain of food and drink pubs, the original Yates's Wine Lodges which proliferated in the North West were real spit-and-sawdust places with no airs and graces. The first Yates's Wine Lodge was opened in Oldham by Peter Yates from Preston, and the Lodges were known for their cheap, sweet, fortified wine from Australia and South Africa. Yates's also invented the 'hot blob', a powerful mix of this sweet, fortified white wine, brandy, hot water, lemon and sugar. They are still selling them today, and for £1.50 you can get a large blob in the Preston Yates's, which has been in the same spot for over a century. The modern recipe is a shot of 'Australian Liqueur Wine', hot water, lemon slices, and brown sugar. It might be a little lighter in alcohol, but it is still heady stuff and perfect for a bitter day.

i OPEN DAILY, SEE WEBSITE FOR OPENING TIMES

⏵ 144-146 CHURCH STREET TEL 01772 556941

@ WWW.WEAREYATES.CO.UK

Winckleys's is the place for a good cup of coffee. It has an impressive coffee machine and a nice upstairs room where you can enjoy a bowl of tasty homemade soup, a filled barm cake, or a platter built around Lancashire cheese or potted shrimps.

i OPEN MON-FRI 8-5, SAT 9.30-5, CLOSED SUN

⏵ 12 WINCKLEY STREET TEL 01772 257725

@ WWW.WINCKLEYS.CO.UK

Winckley News & Copy Shop is opposite Winckley's, its window filled with jars of sweets made by Stockley's (www.stockleys-sweets.co.uk) in nearby Blackburn. To know what has excited generations of local sweet-lovers, you need to try Stockley's Sarsaparilla Drops, Winter Nips, Herbal Candy Cinder Toffee, and 'world-famous' Coltsfoot Rock.

Perambulation

Beyond the main highlights, books, food and drink, there are many more small and interesting details and locations to be enjoyed in passing as you walk from place to place. Architecturally, the centre of Preston has more in common with early nineteenth-century Liverpool than high-Victorian Manchester. There is a sense of spaciousness and graciousness in the wide streets plus an attractive plainness and solid sense of proportion in the houses and terraces. This is warm, red-brick, Lancashire architecture and it's noticeable that doors, entrances and door surrounds are important; they are wonderfully varied, often striking, and usually feature interesting decorative and ornamental details. Here are a few good things to look for:

Make a detour via Chapel Street from Fishergate to see Winckley Square, passing **St Wilfrid's RC Church** (1793) which has a spectacular interior – do look inside if it's open. **Winckley Square** (Preston's 'greatest visual asset' according to Pevsner) is an elegant late Georgian square – actually more a rectangle - which is so large that when the leaves are out on the trees it's difficult to see from end to end. Its lovely red terraces with smart portico doorways enclose an uneven, undulating public park which is the beginning of the long, smooth slope that then becomes Avenham Park and continues down to the river.

Walk on beyond Winckley Square to get to the two parks, Avenham and Miller. If you continue out through the other side of Miller Park you come to **West Cliff** which has some very grand houses and a fine ter-

race which wouldn't look out of place in Hampstead. Just off West Cliff is the very short **North Cliff Street** with nice terraces with very tall doorways and windows. Carry on up to **Fishergate Hill**, turn right towards the railway station, and you'll find more of interest in the domestic buildings here and on the streets off it such as Stanley Place, Walton's Parade and Spring Bank. Close to the station is the large, imposing County Hall (1890s).

Continuing down **Fishergate** from the station, there is a mix of shop fronts from the great to the awful, with signs that Preston had little flings with Art Deco and Sixties modern. The former Woolworth's (now Next) was one of the first in the UK, and the wonderful façade is more what you'd expect to find in a small town in America than in a mill town in Lancashire. The extravagantly tiled and mosaiced, green, white and gold former Booth's grocer's shop is now a Waterstone's; Booth's is a big name here in the North West and its supermarkets are excellent (unfortunately, the Preston stores are not in the centre). At the point where Fishergate becomes Church Street is St John's Minster (1855) which, if open, has a peaceful, gloriously pale interior with a hammerbeam roof painted with strikingly simple, graphic patterns. The play on white, light, and dark with touches of red, grey and gold is very effective, and there is more colour interest in the decent stained glass by William Wailes (1850s, typically brightly coloured with plenty of mauve, blue, green and red) and a nice window under the tower by the Lancaster firm of Shrigley & Hunt (1907) with beautiful fabric details in golds and yellows (page 55). Behind the church on Stoneygate is the First Church of Christ the Scientist (1950, very Fifties glass bricks) with a surprisingly domestic garden (small, beautifully looked after) and Arkwright House (1728), a rare surviving older building which was built for the headmaster of Preston Grammar. Richard Arkwright (born 1732 in Preston) lived here in 1768 while developing his revolutionary spinning machine.

Opposite the Minster at 14-15 Church Street is the **Twelve Tellers**, recently opened by Wetherspoon's in an Edwardian Baroque building, most recently the TSB. It dates from 1905 and was originally the head-quarters of the Preston Savings Bank. It's classic Wetherspoon's, a company that has a great track record of converting large, unconventional premises into pubs (see also the former huge Post Office in Blackburn, now the Postal Order, the Old Chapel (1866, Methodist, ironically) in Darwen, and the fabulous 1920s Art Picture House in Bury). The ornate ceiling in the banking hall has been restored, parts of the counter have been reused, the old marble security gates are in place, and the impressive pendant lights look remarkably similar to those in an old photo showing the twelve bank tellers. It's excellent that these places with often wonderfully interesting and historical interiors are now being adapted and reused and that people have access to what would otherwise be shuttered and closed-off premises. It is to be hoped that the Preston Heritage Investment Strategy enables more of Preston's beautiful old buildings to have a new lease of life.

If you carry on to the end of Church Street and cross the A6, you reach the Museum of Lancashire in what was once the quarter sessions house (built 1825, and explains why Preston Prison is next door). This is a popular, family-friendly place with masses of information and displays crammed in. There is a wonderful late Victorian/Edwardian frying range from an old chippy; it was made by JE Nuttall in Rochdale and features tiles with scenes of lakes, hills and trees. The shop sells Uncle Joe's Mint Balls ('to keep you all aglow') from nearby Wigan.

(Open Tues-Sat 10.30-5, Sun 12-5, www.lancashire.gov.uk/museumo-flancashire).

You may notice the **Preston coat of arms** in many places. The lamb (sitting or standing) is the lamb of St Wilfrid, patron saint of Preston, and the letters 'PP' stand for *Princeps Pacis* ('Prince of Peace') but some like to claim they stand for 'Proud Preston'. The Corn Exchange, Cenotaph, and Town Hall all have good examples of Preston's curly-haired sheep.

And finally, a landmark which is hard to miss: the thin, needle-sharp, and very tall spire of **St Walburge's RC Church** (1854) on Pedder Street to the north-west of the train station. At 309 feet/94 metres this splendid spire is the third tallest in Britain (after Salisbury and Norwich cathedrals) and the tallest of any non-cathedral church. The architect was Joseph Hansom, of Hansom cab fame, and the church is one of his and Preston's greatest buildings (it was given Grade I listing status as long ago as 1950). The interior has a spectacular, steeply-pitched hammerbeam roof, life-size painted statues of saints, a pretty rose window, and is large enough to seat 1,000 people. It has been compared to a medieval hall, is marvellously colourful, and contains lovely, patterned stained glass by Maycock and windows by Hardman of Birmingham. The church narrowly escaped closure in 2014, but was rescued and is now active once again. Apart from daily services, it is possible to visit the church between 11.30 and 2.30 on Saturdays, although the church has plans to open more frequently (check website for details www.stwalburge.org).

Parks, pubs and terraces

To understand Preston, it's necessary to appreciate the importance here of parks, pubs, pies, peas and football (not forgetting Preston Grasshoppers RFC, est. 1869, one of the most brilliantly named rugby union clubs of all). These are all vital components of daily life, together with the local, endearingly daft sense of humour (think of Nick Park, creator of Wallace and Gromit, Leo Baxendale, Beano cartoonist, actor John Inman, and cricketer Andrew Flintoff, all of whom hail from Preston), and they are deeply embedded in the history and character of the city.

Like so many cotton towns and industrial cities of Lancashire, Preston contains several large, municipal parks created by generous benefactors in Victorian times. **Moor Park**, to the north of the city, is Preston's oldest and largest park, laid out in 1833-35 and improved by E Milner in the 1860s in a job creation scheme for unemployed mill workers during the Lancashire Cotton Famine of 1861-65. Over the years it has seen changes, but it has never stopped providing space and facilities for leisure and sport for the people of Preston (this continues today with a large number of courts, greens and pitches). In 2013 the park was given Grade II* listing status, with the accolade of a star because its design is essentially unchanged from its original nineteenth-century layout and the park retains various features, structures and planting, and because of its historic interest as an especially early example of a municipal park. It's a great place for legs, dogs, balls, avenues, fresh air and greenery.

Opposite Moor Park is **Deepdale Stadium**, home of Preston North End FC. It's on what is now called Sir Tom Finney Way in recognition of the eponymous local hero (1922-1914) who was born in a street next to the ground and became the club's – and one of English football's – most famous and well-liked players. The ground was first used for football in 1878 thus making it the world's oldest league football ground in the world. PNE is also famous for its match-day butter pies (filled with onions and potatoes, also available at Preston Market see page 24); when the company that supplied them to the fans went bust in 2008, there was an outcry until a new, local supplier was found. I can't think of anything better than a butter pie to go with a football match, unless it's a mug of hot Bovril (also available at the ground).

On the other side of Moor Park is one of Preston's most famous pubs, variously described as a 'drinking institution', a 'proper local pub', a 'Victorian parlour pub', and an 'iconic boozer'. **The Moorbrook** (370 North Road, tel 01772 823302, open Mon-Sat 12-12, Sun 12-11.30) is all of these things. Its beer credentials are exemplary (real ale, a great list of craft beers) and there's etched glass, dark polished wood, cast iron posts, a warm atmosphere, and food including big pies with peas and gravy (served 12-2 and 5 -7.30). Where once it hosted the Canary Fanciers' Society, it now hosts knitting nights, quiz nights, open mic nights, acoustic nights and sports nights. It's the pub everyone would like to have just around the corner from where they live.

Terraces Nineteenth-century red-brick terraced housing is as much a part of the Lancashire landscape as the hills and valleys, and a good amount has survived in towns such as Oldham, Blackburn, Bolton, Wigan, and Preston. For an idea of just how many terraces once filled the streets, it's worth having a look at the Preston Digital Archive on Flickr which has black and white aerial photos of the area north of Preston city centre taken in the 1920s through to the 1950s: they are utterly fascinating. Laid out below the camera are the huge spinning, weaving and embroidery mills that so dominated the landscape and the working life here, and all around the mills and the spiky spires of the churches are lines and lines of neat terraced housing, like a carefully constructed model or very crowded Monopoly board. Looking at them, you begin to get an idea of the sheer scale of the cotton enterprise, the phenomenal planning, energy, money and building that characterised the Victorian age, and the impact these had on the urban landscape.

Unlike some of the major industrial towns in Britain which swept away virtually all of their Victorian terraces in massive and often controversial clearance programmes, Preston halted the demolition plans in the 1960s and thus managed to retain many of its nineteenth-century street patterns and terraces. The geometric grid and ladder layouts remain and can be clearly seen in colour on today's aerial photos via Google Earth, and at street level. One day, these sorts of places may well be heritage sites, but for now it's worth appreciating a city that hasn't rushed to remove something that works well and is still going strong – in the same way it has retained parched peas, butter pies, and local shops.

The best area for these red-brick terraces – even the most humble have nice details and an amazing variety of styles of doorways – is the arc to the north of the centre, above the A59/A6 ring road and below Blackpool Road (the A5085). Plungington (west of Garstang Road and south of Blackpool Road) has terraces from the 1880s – now often occupied by students – and to the east of Garstang Road and south of Moor

Park, are more terraces, often with good proportions and tall, grand doorways. Between the two developments is the enormous church of St Thomas (designed by Edward Welby Pugin, some of Augustus Pugin, opened 1867, and extended in 1888, no doubt to accommodate the growing population), to the west is Tulketh Mill (1905), one of the few surviving cotton mills, and scattered about are former corner shops, often with a door set on a diagonal, and pubs. It's a living lesson in the social history of Preston.

As well as the bright-red brick terraces built for mill workers, Preston has some well-preserved earlier terraces which accommodated Prestonians such as a local printer/bookseller and Joseph Livesey who founded the Temperance Movement (he lived at 13 Bank Parade). There is a cluster of streets to the east of Winckley Square and Miller Park and close to the river in which many of the houses are listed because they are parts of formerly complete sets of this type of late Georgian housing. They are built with a paler, pinkish-red brick and have nice stone dressings, doorways, steps, sash windows, and some retain original features inside such as cellars, service staircases, and fires. These are old residential streets with character, history and architectural variety, from the period when Preston was already enjoying fast growth due to the development from the 1780s onwards of the cotton industry. A walk round Bushell Place, Latham Street, Frenchwood Street and Bairstow Street – the latter with good cobbles – will take in 1830s terraces while Great Avenham Street is earlier (c1825) and Avenham Road one of the earliest (c1815-20).

Blackburn

With its enormous Bus Station (and busy railway station), Preston is tremendously well-connected, and a fine starting point for many trips and jaunts to the seaside and surrounding parts of Lancashire. It makes sense, then, to include some of the best places that can be reached within an hour by bus (or train or car). This way you can experience the Bus Station as it was intended to be used, as part of a busy bus hub.

Blackburn is just ten miles east of Preston, and it takes around 20 minutes to reach by direct train or approximately 40 minutes by bus from Preston Bus station to Blackburn railway station.

Unless you already know it, it's easy to imagine that the whole of the North West is covered in cotton towns with barely a blade of grass between them. But if you travel between Preston and Blackburn you are swiftly pitched into the scenic and dramatic East Lancashire Hills landscape between the two. This hilliness continues into the town which is full of steep slopes; standing in the centre you can see long, straight roads with terraced houses almost sitting one of top of the other, running up and away towards the surrounding hills and ridges which are clearly visible and very much part of the town's setting and scenery.

Blackburn is a very old town and its history of textile manufacturing goes back to the thirteenth century. In the seventeenth century it was famous for its 'Blackburn checks' and 'Blackburn greys' fabrics, and by the eighteenth-century textiles were the main industry. From then until the mid-twentieth century, it grew into the 'weaving capital of the world' with a huge boom in the nineteenth century. Eventually, its over-reliance on cotton meant it suffered - and continues to suffer - from the effects of the UK textile industry's post-war decline.

Now that the mills and looms have gone, Blackburn is left with a post-industrial landscape of great potential. The terraces, the imposing Victorian churches, the grand Old Town Hall (1850s), the former Technical School (1888, exuberant, florid brick and yellow terracotta) and the Baroque old Post Office (1907, now a Wetherspoon's) are relics of an era of civic pride and confidence, but life continues, and adaptations and changes are being made.

There are many good reasons to visit Blackburn. Come for the Lancashire hills, the Dorothy Whipple connections, the cathedral and its modern fixtures and stained glass, for the crocuses in spring and the sarsaparilla and tripe at the market, for one of the best railway glass canopies you'll ever stand under, and one of the grandest glasshouses you'll find in a municipal park. Eat locally made sweets, buy a sewing machine, have a butty and a brew in a café, see excellent post-war stained glass and sculpture, admire the wonderful Arts & Crafts entrance to the Museum and Art Gallery, and stretch your legs on the slopes.

Dorothy Whipple, together with Alfred Wainwright, Kathleen Ferrier, Russell Harty and Wayne Hemingway, is one of the most distinguished people to come from Blackburn. But only she captured the topography, character, the way of life and patterns of speech and preserved them in her wonderful, immensely readable and deeply humane novels and short stories. She was born here in 1893, the daughter of

Walter Stirrup, a local architect (he designed the Fire Station in Byrom Street, completed early 1920s, and he had an office on Richmond Terrace, the most elegant terrace in Blackburn). She grew up and went to school here, but moved to Nottinghamshire after her marriage in 1917. When her husband died, she spent her last years in Blackburn and died in 1966. By then, her wise, beautifully observed novels of family life had fallen out of favour with the reading public, but thankfully they have been rediscovered and republished by Persephone Books (www. perspephonebooks.co.uk).

Dorothy Whipple is marvellous on character and the textures of domestic life, and two of her books are worth reading in the Blackburn context. *High Wages* (1930) is the story of a young girl who works in a draper's and moves on to setting up her own dress shop, located in a town square which could be Blackburn (before alterations) or a composite of several Lancashire towns, including Preston. But Blackburn is where you can picture Jane walking up a steep hill to fit the dreadful Mrs Greenwood with her stays, and going off more happily into the surrounding countryside to enjoy the bracing winds and open spaces. (In the Preface to the Persephone edition of 2009, I wrote that the novel is a 'celebration of the Lancastrian values of hard work and stubbornness, and there could be no finer setting for a shop-girl-made-good story, than the county in which cotton was king'.) *Greenbanks* (1932) is influenced by Dorothy Whipple's own upbringing, family homes, and her relationship with her Blackburn grandmother. The park that features in the book could well be Corporation Park in Blackburn, opened 1857, an outstanding example of landscaping and a fine, Victorian municipal with a triumphal archway entrance, formal gardens, fountains, war memorial, two lakes, two porter's lodges, an aviary, a 1900 glass and iron Conservatory, tennis courts and fine views south to the West Pennine Moors. For a more personal impression of Blackburn through the eyes of the author as child in the late nineteenth- and early twentieth-century, it's worth reading *Another Day* (1936) if you can track down a copy, as it is full of local detail and character. To picture the settings, it helps to know where Dorothy Whipple lived; there is a blue plaque on 9 Edgeware Road where she was born, and she subsequently lived at Elm Bank on St Silas's Road and at Hawthorns on Duke's Brow, all of which are in the hilly north-west part of the town, not far from the Blackburn Golf Club, of which her father was a founding member.

Blackburn Station is a fine, solid 1888 station with a superb glass canopy to shelter passengers and meeters and greeters from the Lancashire rain and weather. It's a spectacular piece of glazing, with twenty roof spans, latticed girders, and a fretted wooden valance. It's one of the details that make train travel so enjoyable. The station's recent renovations and works are part of a bigger, ongoing development of Blackburn's 'Cathedral Quarter' – and you can't miss the cathedral on arrival because it is directly opposite the station.

Blackburn Cathedral is one of the newest English cathedrals but is, in fact, a mix of old and modern. The nave is what was a pretty, pale pink sandstone 'Strawberry Hill'/Georgian Gothic parish church built in 1826 (you see quite a few churches in this style in the North West) which was declared a cathedral in 1926. As a result it was enlarged and, in a very clever post-war grafting job, a new section with its distinctive lantern and spire (1967) was added on. You can see the joins, so to speak, from the outside, but inside it all fits and works together so well as a whole that they are barely noticeable.

And the interior is really what makes Blackburn cathedral so surprising and interesting. The visitor is immediately struck by the pale interior, with its tall, simplified Gothic painted ceiling, flooded with light, immaculately maintained, incredibly tidy, sparkling and gleaming. The mix of the arching, elegant Georgian part with the post-war, Festival of Britain spiky aesthetic, careful choice of paint colour and high quality materials such as highly polished Derbyshire limestone make the cathedral breathtaking yet peaceful. It is not plain, but it is simply done, and is adorned with some really some stunning pieces of modern art in the form of stained glass, etched glass, corona, six-winged seraphs and sculpture, all by John Hayward (1929-2007) who worked with the cathedral for many years from the 1970s to the 1990s. Look, for example, at his wonderful abstract stained glass window (1970) in organic hues of greens browns and yellows in St Martin's Chapel, and examine his window in the south transept which contains masses of fragments of Victorian glass from the windows that were in the nave of the old church set into a very modern style (lots of little angel faces peeping out). The latter also contains the glass from one of two windows designed by Edward Burne-Jones for the church; the second was not broken up, and has been moved a position behind the cathedra, near the Jesus Chapel. For more information about the building, fittings and details, it's worth picking up a copy of the excellent and well-illustrated guide to the Cathedral by Canon Chris Chivers which is sold in the shop downstairs next to the Café in the Crypt.

i OPEN DAILY, TIMES VARY, CHECK WEBSITE

▶ CATHEDRAL CLOSE TEL 01254 503090

@ WWW.BLACKBURNCATHEDRAL.COM

John Hayward
1970

Blackburn Museum & Art Gallery You may not know it, but Blackburn has two nationally important collections. One is the RE Hart bequest, the gift from a local rope-maker of 8,000 coins, manuscripts, and books which cannot be matched outside London, and the other is the outstanding TB Lewis collection of Japanese woodblock prints. Then there is the Egyptology room (made possible by John Garstang who was an eminent archaeologist from Blackburn), drawers and drawers of beetles and bugs, various stuffed birds, a room full of Blackburn-made looms and examples of the clogs worn by mill-workers, and a fine South Asian gallery. What is lacking, perhaps, is the art, although the staircase is hung with Victorian oils and there are several paintings dotted about, and what is out on display does of course depend on the gallery's programme at the time of visiting. It would be nice, for instance, to see works from the gallery's good number of twentieth-century paintings by artists, often local, who may not now be terribly well-known, but who, in their time, were bright stars and exponents of an influential post-war style (for example Peter Shackleton and David Wild, both from Blackburn, and Malcolm Fryer and Michael Buhler).

However, there is a bonus in that this is a gallery worth visiting as much for the building itself and its fantastically preserved-in-aspic porch and entrance area, as for its displays and laudable determination to engage with its visitors. The original edifice was built 1872-4 in a free Gothic style, but it was enlarged and altered in the 1890s which is when the Arts & Crafts detailing was added. It is like stepping back in time as you pass through wrought-iron gates bearing marvellous, emerald-green scroll signs with lovely Aesthetic lettering, and a tiled porch with two fabulous pictorial panels showing four women – Science (yes, a woman having a light-bulb moment) and Labour, Painting and Poetry. The entrance hall itself is richly green and gold, with wrought-iron balustrading on a solidly Victorian staircase. It may not be to your taste, but it is certainly impressively old-fashioned and crowded, and a distinct contrast to modern white-walled, tastefully minimalist galleries.

On the building's exterior are carved bas-relief panels by CW Searle, added during the extension work. If you stand on Richmond Terrace (1838, listed, very desirable properties) you can see four panels which reflect late nineteenth-century interests illustrated with contemporary figures. They are dated and no doubt suspect in many ways, but they are of their moment, and represent Victorian Commerce, Textiles, Iron Founding and Agriculture. The Museum Street panels show figures in ancient and medieval costume representing Art, Literature, and Science.

Provincial galleries and museums like this are to be applauded for their tenacity and their sterling work with schools and the local community. But they are also guardians and keepers of publicly-owned art and collections, and it is worth remembering that many treasures may be discovered in the very places you might not expect to find them.

i FREE ENTRY, OPEN TUES-SAT 10-4.45

MUSEUM STREET TEL 01254 667130

@ WWW.BLACKBURNMUSEUM.ORG.UK

Blackburn Market has a long history and is now an indoor market in a new building, opened in 2011. It's one of many excellent Lancashire markets (see also Preston Market on page 24, and Bury Market if you are in the area and/or are a lover of black pudding). It's worth dropping in for several reasons. First, you can get tripe from the Tripe Stall which also sells cowheel and black pudding. Secondly, there is an Oddie's bakery stand where you can have a cup of tea and a jam slice or an iced bun. Thirdly, at Spuds 'n' Puds they still sell sarsaparilla (one of the non-alcoholic brews of the Temperance Movement) and parched peas (see page 48 and page 108).

Then there is Stockley's. Stockley's (www.stockleys-sweets.co.uk, see also page 49), based in Blackburn, has been making confectionery since 1918. It has all the sweet favourites of yesteryear and a few classic specialities, such as Sarsaparilla Sticks and Drops, and Coltsfoot Rock which is unique to the company, a brittle confection made with icing sugar and flavoured with a plant with hoof-shaped leaves. And, still going strong despite the lack of miners these days, are packs of 'Miner's Mate', charmingly described as 'bronchial lozenges', made with natural flavourings such as clove, aniseed and peppermint.

ⓘ OPEN MON-SAT 8.30-5.30

⟫ CHURCH STREET TEL 01254 669258

@ WWW.BLACKBURNMARKET.COM

Sewing machines Fittingly, Blackburn is home to **Hobkirks** which holds the largest stock of sewing machines in the UK, including all the major names and models. The HQ is on Darwen Street where they sell and repair domestic sewing machines, and hold classes. There is also a lovely little private museum of a hundred or so sewing machines - most of which are more than a hundred years old - collected by the chairman. These often beautiful and sometimes ornately decorated machines tell a whole history of home stitching, dress-making and mending. If you'd like the history explained, visit by appointment, otherwise ask in the shop if it's possible to see the machines.

i OPEN MON-FRI 9-5.30, SAT 9-4.30

▶ 120-128 DARWEN STREET TEL 01254 693555

@ WWW.HOBKIRK.CO.UK

If you looking for fine fabrics at decent prices, go to **Standfast & Barracks**, the well-known fabric printers on the northern outskirts of Lancaster. They have a famously good factory shop selling discontinued fabrics, eg Sanderson, Morris & Co, Designers Guild, Liberty, and seconds (open Mon-Fri 9.30-1, Sat 10-2, Caton Road, Lancaster, tel 01524 840500, www.standfast-barracks.com).

The Café in the Crypt in the cathedral serves decent, plain breakfasts and lunches in a spacious room. It's friendly and warm, and a good place to get a sandwich or a bowl of soup. Open Tues-Sat 9-3. The best coffee is to be found at **Exchange Coffee** in the old Exchange Arcade (1848). It's a shop and a café (part of a small group in the North West) with a nice, cosy, old, wood-panelled coffee-house feel.

i OPEN MON-SAT 9-5.30

▶ 13-15 FLEMING SQUARE TEL 01254 54258

@ WWW.EXCHANGECOFFEE.CO.UK

Map and town trails A good map and two useful, informative Town Trails (North and South) are available from the Blackburn Visitor Centre, 50-54 Church Street, tel: 01254 688040, open Mon-Fri 9-5, Sat 9.30-4. Or download from the website www.visitblackburn.co.uk.

Southport

Southport is on the edge of the flat, black, fertile, West Lancashire coastal plain which, with its drainage ditches, canals, vegetables – very good carrots - and market gardens, looks from the train not a little unlike Holland. Historically, and perhaps temperamentally, it belonged to Lancashire but it is now a part of the Metropolitan Borough of Sefton. It developed as a resort from the end of the eighteenth century, went through a period of great growth and prosperity in the Victorian age with another stylish peak in the 1930s, and has never lost its appeal or character. This is partly because it is also a popular residential town, something that enables Southport to weather difficult times more easily than seaside resorts which rely heavily on tourism, and partly because the town has invested well in upkeep and attractions, making efforts to maintain character and quality without compromising the essential, much-loved character of the place.

It is Southport's famous air of gentility and smartness that makes it different. It has never been a kiss-me-quick resort, but has always presented itself as a cut above and rather select. And, anyway, people have come for reasons other than cheerfully noisy day trips. The resort made its name based on its fresh, clean sea air, and it has attracted those in need of rest and recuperation (and golf); the handsome, low Convalescent Hospital was built as early as 1806 with the red-brick, Gothic Southport Promenade Hospital next door coming later (1850s), both of which demonstrated the belief in the town's health-giving benefits.

Today, Southport is still renowned for its elusive tide, vast stretches of clean sandy beach (and a long, long walk for a paddle) and sand dunes which make it a haven for many examples of flora and fauna and birds, Lord Street with its glass canopies and iron columns, golf at nearby Royal Birkdale Golf Club, the annual Southport Flower show, one of the longest piers in the country (1859, with a little tram to help you travel the length and a Pavilion at the end for refreshments above the sea) and bracing walks. It also has a brilliant art gallery and cultural hub, a superb independent bookshop, tasty fish and chips, and a surprising Arts & Crafts church with lovely stained glass.

It is also just fifteen miles to the north of Crosby beach where you will find of the most amazing permanent sculpture installations. This is Antony Gormley's 'Another Place' (1997) which consists of a hundred cast-iron, life-size figures spread out along two miles of the foreshore, with some going half a mile out to sea (with warnings as this is a non-bathing beach).

Lord Street Southport's railway station is set a little way back from the long, straight Lord Street which dominates Southport. The 1852 train shed is airy, bright, glass and iron, but the modern frontage with enormous Southport letters is quite out of keeping with the area it serves. It's a short walk to Lord Street and the two pavilions of the 1923 War Memorial. Looking either way from this point along the wide boulevard, you cannot fail to take in the famous glass canopies supported by iron posts with a huge variety of decorative wrought-iron work (they are also often described as verandahs).

Lord Street was begun in 1820 and it developed in a planned way, although it contains a fascinating range of architectural styles, tiles, terracotta, mock Tudor beams, carved stone, and history. With its bandstand, gardens, pavilions, cafés, hotels, shops, arcades, former cinemas, and churches, this is a richly interesting streetscape. It's striking how many toy shops there are for young holiday-makers, especially in the nice, cramped Royal Arcade and smart, bright Wayfarers Arcade, and if you want to play bingo at Mecca Bingo, you get the added bonus of the seeing the magnificent former Garrick Theatre at close quarters. When it was built in 1932, it was the epitome of theatrical and cinematic glamour with an ultra-modish Art Deco/Egyptian design, much of which is still intact inside.

Lord Street is a lovely place to stroll with regular stops to look up, and it is worth picking up a copy of the Southport Town Trail produced by the Southport Civic Society (www.southportcivicsociety.com) from The Atkinson for more detailed information about its buildings.

The Atkinson Right in the centre of Lord Street is the Atkinson, originally opened in 1878 as the Atkinson Art Gallery & Library, built with money donated by William Atkinson, a cotton manufacturer whose wife was often ill and spent much time in Southport. Now it is simply 'The Atkinson', a new incarnation which was opened in 2013 to great acclaim, flying in the face of all the doom and gloom about culture and cuts. The Victorian buildings have been beautifully renovated, repurposed and cleverly stitched together so that movement around the various floors and rooms is easy and well-planned. It still has old tiles and a huge fireplace and a grand staircase in the entrance hall, and the original proportions and many details have been kept. But at the same time, the interior has been opened up and adapted in order to offer a mix of art, performance, literature, and music. The Atkinson is now a library, a museum, a gallery, a theatre, a shop, a café and a bakery, a Tourist Information Office and a booking office. It manages to combine all these brilliantly, and is smart, welcoming and unstuffy. It must be the envy of many other provincial towns.

The art is, as you might hope, a real strength, and the gallery has plenty to choose from in what is a fantastic collection for a relatively small town. Some of the 'interpretive texts' (ie the information next to a painting) are open to debate, and what you see will depend on when you visit, but it will be nicely displayed in a gallery that feels fresh and lively and down-to-earth. Its real strength is the twentieth century, especially the first half, and there are some delightful paintings from this period such as *Blackberries* (1922) by Harold Harvey, *Suffolk Pastoral* (1920) by Philip Connard (a famous local name) and *The Lark* (1912) by George Henry. There is a really good collection of flower paintings (eg by Adrain Berg, Frank Brangwyn, Duncan Grant, Philip Connard) and an outstanding mix of portraits, plus a general roll-call of famous names of twentieth-century painting: Charles Ginner, Sickert and Steer, Munnings and Lowry, Augustus John, Vanessa Bell, Laura Knight, William Orpen, Carel Weight, Sheila Fell, Anne Redpath, John Piper and John Bellany. There are a few earlier paintings (William Etty, John William Waterhouse and assorted *genre* painters) plus a small number of pieces of good sculpture by Moore, Hepworth and Frink. What makes the Atkinson all the more refreshing is that is has some fine work by lesser-known artists which means you see something a little bit different and come across some nice surprises.

The museum tells the story of Southport, the highlight of which may well be the Dan Dare display. Frank Hampson, the creator of the 1950s science fiction hero whose adventures appeared in the *Eagle* comic, lived in Southport (the *Eagle* itself was founded by a Southport vicar), which explains the wealth of Dan Dare material, including busts of the hero with cap and his fantastically large and chiselled chin.

The café is a nice buzzy place to sit and enjoy what comes out of the bakery next door, and is excellent for drinks, meals and snacks. It is a modern version of the old style tea rooms that were once part of Southport (several still exist, such as the Westminster Tea Rooms at 165 Lord Street) but never have any of them come with so many cultural riches.

i THE ATKINSON: OPEN MON-FRI 9.30-5, SUN 11-3

    MUSEUM AND GALLERIES: OPEN MON-SAT 10-4, SUN 11-3

▶ LORD STREET TEL 01704 533333

@ WWW.THEATKINSON.CO.UK

The Promenade is much altered on the sea side, but on the town side you can still see what remains from the days when visitors came to Southport to recover and recuperate. At the north end is the bright red, former Southport Promenade Hospital and the Convalescent Hospital next door (the days of 'convalescence' are sadly long gone). A short way further down, at the corner with Nevill Street, were the famous Victoria Salt Water Baths in famously elegant premises. These were built in 1871 with a long French/Classical front and the promise of no fewer than six pools inside to attract tourists. One part of the building is still a leisure centre with three pools, and although most of the interior is much altered, the former men's first class pool retains the original roof

VICTORIA
SEA WATER
BATHS
ENTIRELY NEW
TURKISH

PLEASANT BOOKS
· FOR · THE ·
CHILDREN

with Victorian ironwork, and there is still an eye-catching tiled wall sign advertising 'Entirely New Turkish, Russian & Swimming Baths – Finest in District'.

Books *Broadhurst's Bookshop* is, undoubtedly, the type of bookshop a committed book-buyer searches for and rarely finds. It has been open since 1920, in a mid-nineteenth century terrace with obligatory glass canopy just off Lord Street, and has very imaginatively themed window displays. Inside, there are four floors of new and second-hand books in a series of numbered rooms. The building was originally housing, and retains some original domestic features such as steep stairs, old doors, large windows overlooking the street, fireplaces and bells. This, with the deep green woodwork, dark bookshelves and glass cases, chairs, and open fire on the ground floor make it delightfully old-fashioned and atmospheric, a bookshop from another era as the old painted signs suggest (it's very easy to imagine Dorothy Whipple's novels selling well here to the readers of Southport). It stocks a fantastic range of new and second-hand books in the carefully categorized, neat, and tidy rooms. Best of all, your book purchases will be wrapped in brown paper and string pulled from the original string holder - just one of the many good reasons to browse and buy here.

i OPEN MON-SAT 9-5.30, CLOSED SUN

▶ 5-7 MARKET STREET   TEL 01704 532064/534110

@ WWW.CKBROADHURST.CO.UK

There is a branch of *Waterstones* at 367 Lord Street (open Mon-Sat 9.30-5.30, Sun 11-5) in the former National and Provincial Bank (1925-27).

Flowers June the Florist sells flowers from premises at 108 Lord Street (www.junetheflorist.co.uk) which have barely changed since the shop was established in 1925. The curved plate glass, the canopy, the wide pavement filed with flowers and, above, the huge 1920s gold, cursive 'June' sign make you want to buy something, even if it is just a bunch of daffodils.

Nearby, at the entrance to the recently refurbished indoor Market and next to Mrs G The Greengrocer's which sells local Lancashire produce, is a colourful and profusely stocked flower stall (www.purefloraldesign.co.uk).

Stained glass Holy Trinity Church which was built 1895-1913 is a lovely surprise here in the North West, where churches are often of the severe Victorian Gothic with pointy spire variety. Its unusual, tall, red brick and Portland stone tower can be seen from the train and as you emerge from the railway station, contrasting with the rest of the town and piquing curiosity. It is well worth satisfying that curiosity by going inside, because you will find an enormous, extremely wide, pink sand-stone interior with a soaringly high barrel-vaulted roof. It is really pretty amazing, and it must have impressed many a visiting holiday-maker for whom going to church was (is) part of the town's offering.

The architect was Huon Matear of Liverpool who described the style as 'a free treatment of the late Decorated Period' (ie the dominant style of church architecture in England in the mid-fourteenth century), but it now appears to be a very Arts & Crafts take on this style. Indeed, many of the furnishings were made by members of the Bromsgrove Guild of Arts & Crafts (1898-1966) who were responsible for the beautiful,

intricate wood carving (eg pulpit, screen, reredos) as well as the ears of corn over the north door.

The church also contains some very good twentieth-century stained glass. In the south aisle is a fascinating, richly detailed, Morris-influenced memorial window by Barraclough and Sanders to Lieutenant Eric Wood who was killed at Ypres in 1916. Of great interest are the 1914 window by Wilhelmina Geddes, very high up in the chancel, and the four Sir Galahad/Holy Grail windows (1917) in the Lady Chapel by AJ Davies of the Bromsgrove Guild. These are a memorial to two soldiers with sweetly youthful faces who were killed in 1915, guarded by angels who look as though they have just stepped off the cover of a contemporary romantic novel or out of an advert for soap.

This is a fine gallery of arts and crafts, carving and lettering, mostly paid for by generous local benefactors such as Mr and Mrs Elder of the then-famous Elder Dempster Shipping Line and Joseph Dewhurst of Dewhurst cotton mills and thread, which explains the 'best of everything' approach and the church's unified style.

i OPEN WEEKDAYS 10.30-12 AND 2-2.30

▶ CORNER OF HOUGHTON STREET AND MANCHESTER ROAD

@ WWW.HOLYTRINITYSOUTHPORT.ORG.UK

Refreshments At **The Swan** the fish price includes chips and mushy peas and a round of bread and butter and a pot of tea, so you know you are going to get the full works. This family-owned eat-in/take-out place has not changed much in 35 years, and is very popular, friendly and fast.

And you can have a Heinz sponge pudding with custard afterwards. Chippy heaven.

i OPEN FOR LUNCH AND DINNER DAILY, TIMES MAY VARY ACCORDING TO SEASON

⟫ 52-54 STANLEY STREET, OR ACCESS FROM LORD STREET VIA A PASSAGE TO THE SIDE OF BOLD HOTEL TEL 01704 530720

@ WWW.THESWANRESTAURANT.CO.UK

Tappers Café & Bar does exuberantly generous, home-made cakes decorated and finished with lavish amounts of sweets, chocolates, fillings and toppings. This independent café is run by two sisters, and is well-known for its good breakfasts, lunches, and snacks.

i OPEN MON-THURS 9-4, FRI 6-6.30, SAT 9-4, SUN 10-4

⟫ 9 UNION STREET TEL 01704 539567

@ WWW.TAPPERSCAFE.CO.UK

Stay There is no shortage of hotels in Southport. *The Scarisbrick* (1890-91) and *The Prince of Wales* (1876-7) are the two grand old names, now owned by Britannia Hotels. *The Vincent* (opened 2008) at 98 Lord Street is Southport's most contemporary and stylish hotel (www.thevincenthotel.com).

Map Collect a town map from Visitor Information in The Atkinson, Lord Street, open Mon-Sat 9.30-5, Sun 11-4, tel 01704 533333, www.visitsouthport.com.

Morecambe

When coming to Morecambe, expectations have to be managed, as they say. On cold days the biting winds and boarded-up properties, the betting shops and pound shops, and the gloomy effects of unemployment can no doubt get the better of even the most optimistic and positive visitor. But locals are loyal, and many visitors come here for their annual, much looked-forward-to holidays with a determination to have a good time and enjoy themselves - and they succeed. So make a little effort and visit the Moderne Midland Hotel, browse for books, buy sticks of rude rock from the Rock Shop, eat fish and chips on the front, listen to George Formby tribute acts, and enjoy hot toasted tea-cakes and lots of cups of tea in a time-capsule café.

The town Morecambe was little more than a fishing village, originally called Poulton-le-Sands, until the railway arrived in 1846 (the vestiges of the old Poulton can be found in the area around Poulton Square which is home to the Shrimp Shop). It's a resort created by the Victorians who built the grand Morecambe Promenade station right by the huge, sweeping, sandy Morecambe Bay (they renamed the town after it) and brought hordes of day-trippers and holiday-makers to the fresh salty, breezy Lancashire seaside. Unlike Blackpool which has always been popular with visitors from Lancashire and Manchester and because of its historical railway connections, Morecambe's visitors have tradition¬ally come from Yorkshire, especially the West Riding towns. This explains why Alan Bennett spent many holidays here as a child, listening to conversations in hotels and picking up the wonderful cadences

and turns of phrase that are such a part of his work. (He wrote *Sunset Across the Bay* (1975), a TV play set here, and several wonderful parts for Thora Hird, who came from Morecambe.)

Morecambe was a popular and busy resort until the 1960s when it started to suffer in competition with package holidays and the decline began, although it has continued to be a holiday destination with reduced attractions (the two piers, the various Moderne cinemas, and the huge 1936 Swimming Stadium/lido have gone, and the Winter Gardens no longer functions fully as an entertainment venue). Nevertheless, it's not all gloom and greyness. Here are the things that might bring you sunshine in Morecambe, as Eric Morecambe would say, the things that make Morecambe worth visiting.

The Bay Morecambe's most important asset is its topography. The Bay is five miles long, a huge sweep of sand and mudflats, the largest intertidal area in Britain, where you can see and hear oystercatchers, knots and redshanks, and where fish and tiny brown shrimps are caught, peeled and potted. It's vast, flat, pale, and curved, and is great for walks and fresh air, with lovely views to the north of the Lakeland hills and fells.

Birds All along the sea front you will encounter sculptures of birds: birds on fences, on rocks, on plinths, on an electricity substation, 'bird bollards', and birds at the entrance to Morrison's supermarket. These and more bird-related details scattered about, are all part of the Tern Project (www.lancaster.gov.uk/tern) which was instigated after the town's front had been battered and breached by severe storms over a period of twenty years. There was a huge civil engineering project to make improvements to the promenade and sea defences and to build protection, and the local council decided to link it to a programme of public art. So there are cormorants, razorbills, coots, magpies, mallards and many more, and it's all cheerful and nicely done, not all serious and earnest or Hitchockian, and always with a touch of cartoon character and seaside humour. As well as amusing and adorning, it is also helps to build awareness of Morecambe as nature reserve, and not just a kiss-me-quick resort. There is a Tern Trail leaflet which is worth picking up from the Tourist Information Office at the old railway station opposite the Midland Hotel.

Stone Jetty The Stone Jetty has long been a feature of the Bay, even more so now that the two piers have been lost. It was a railway terminus and wharf for Irish and Scottish and Isle of Man and Barrow ferries - the little building on it is the old station (c1853, now listed) and there used to be goods warehouses and sheds crowded onto the jetty at one time. The lighthouse at the end was built in c1855 (also listed). The jetty is all that is now left of what was Morecambe Harbour; nowadays it is part of the coastal defence works. It features a number of artworks, mostly on the ground in the form of a circular word search containing 70 words, a maze, a hopscotch area, a compass, and is good for a stroll, children, and a look out to sea.

The Midland Hotel is the reason why many people visit Morecambe. They come to see, and perhaps stay in, one of the best, most sleek and elegant examples of Streamline Moderne architecture to be found any-where in the country. It was designed by Oliver Hill who also built a number of simple, very purist, white Art Deco buildings in Frinton, in Essex. Amazingly, it's a railway hotel, built by the London, Midland & Scottish Railway, although it's far removed from the usual and more

typical, solid Victorian variety. In fact, it replaced a hotel of exactly this type, and when it opened in 1933 its modernity and exciting design made all the headlines. As with many Moderne buildings, its time as a cutting-edge hotel was brief, and it became a hospital during the war, was sold in the early 1950s, compromised in the 1960s, and by the 1970s it was very run-down. Eventually, it was all but abandoned despite support from a group of enthusiasts, and it was only when Urban Splash stepped in, bought, renovated and reopened it in 2008, that it was brought back to something approaching its original glory.

The exterior is the ultimate in cool, understated glamour: sparklingly white, curving outwards for the best uninterrupted sea views, and with a stunning entrance with seahorses above carved by Eric Gill. Inside it's a delight, and the staff are very nice about non-residents having a look round the entrance area; it's not possible to go very far unless you are staying or using the bar or restaurant, but you can certainly see enough to impress and to reassure yourself that this Modernist masterpiece is in good nick, as are its famous works of art. Look down at the wonderful Marion Dorn-designed rugs and mosaic seahorse (a motif that is repeated, for example at the end of the staircase hand-rail), look up at the ceiling with its Neptune and Triton medallion by Eric Gill, take in one of the best spiral staircases you'll ever see (perfect for a grand, film star entrance), and look behind the desk at the fantastic, huge bas-relief by Eric Gill of Odysseus being welcomed from the sea by Nausicaa. If you ask, and are lucky, you might be able to see the Eric Gill's beautifully carved and illustrated map of the North West in what was the 'children's room' (a sign of the times: the Liverpool RC cathedral he depicts is based on the Edwin Lutyens' design which was never completed).

If you decide to eat or drink in the Rotunda Bar and Terrace Café (open 12-11pm, good for tea, coffee and drinks, potted shrimps, fish and chips, and 'Lancashire Tapas'), you will be able to see the mural that has been created recently in homage to the short-lived 'Noon and Night' murals by Eric Ravilious and Tirzah Garwood in what were originally the tea rooms. The curved Sun Terrace extension was a later addition and has been retained by Urban Splash, and it is now the place to be seen taking afternoon tea.

There is plenty of literature on the Midland. For a full history, read *The Midland Hotel: Morecambe's Great White Hope* (2008) by Barry Guise and Pam Brook, or buy the very useful booklet *Midland Confidential* by Peter Wade (£2 from the Tourist Information Office) to help you when looking. Peter Wade is also the author of another useful booklet *Echoes of Art Deco* (£2 from the Tourist Information Office) which looks at the town in the 1930s, a period of hope, expansion and prosperity which led to a significant number of Moderne buildings in addition to the Midland (Woolworth's, Burton's, cafés and cinemas, and the immense lido). Morecambe had a few years of glamour and glory when it blew away the last bits of Victorian and Edwardian fustiness, fussiness and ornament, but sadly the war intervened and the moment was gone.

▶ MARINE ROAD WEST   TEL 01524 424000

@ WWW.ENGLISHLAKES.CO.UK

Morecambe Bay Potted Shrimps Potting is a traditional way of preserving meat or fish by sealing it under a layer of fat such as butter (potted meat from a good Lancashire producer is fantastic, especially on a soft, new barm cake). The small brown shrimps are cleaned, cooked and potted locally using butter and spice, often mace, and are delicious on thin slices of hot, toasted brown bread. Baxters have been producing potted shrimps since the 1880s and are generally seen as the top name, or look for the Furness Fish brand which is available in Booths supermarkets (both companies also do mail order). Such is the importance of shrimps to the town, Morecambe FC are known as the 'Shrimps' and wear a shrimp on the club badge on their strip. Baxters has a shop on Thornton Road (behind the Spar) in Morecambe.

i OPEN MON-THURS 9-4.30, FRI 9-1, SAT BY APPOINTMENT)

➤ TEL 01524 410910

@ WWW.BAXTERSPOTTEDSHRIMPS.CO.UK

FURNESS WEBSITE: WWW.MORECAMBEBAYPOTTEDSHRIMPS.COM

The Old Station and Platform The imposing former Morecambe Promenade Station (1907) stands opposite the Midland Hotel (1933), a contrast so stark that it's hard to believe the same railway company was responsible for both within a period of just 26 years. It closed in 1994 and has now been converted into an entertainment hub with a pub and restaurant, but it has retained many original features and still looks like the low, wide, stone, early Tudorbethan station it once was, and it still has a lovely iron and glass porte-cochère. These days, it hosts summer afternoon concerts, and dancing and music outside.

Brucciani's opened in 1939 as a milk bar, and has barely altered since. It is now recognised as one of Britain's classic cafés, sought out and treasured by those who appreciated its wonderful 'high street deco' interior and virtually unchanged menu. It is full of period detail such as ziggurats, chrome, beautifully designed window fittings, glass etched with Venice canal scenes, masses of wood panelling, mirrors, utilitarian caff tables and chairs, a lovely original hatch, and a counter and serving area which appears to be stuck in a time-warp. Brucciani's is the place to come on a cold or wet or grey day for a pot of tea and several hot, buttered tea-cakes (they fly out of the hatch) on old Brucciani's china. You can still have Horlicks which has been on the menu since the café opened or, if you're feeling frivolous and in holiday mood, have the sort of Knickerbocker Glory you expect at the British seaside: tall and filled with whipped cream and ice cream and rivulets of sweet red sauce.

Come out of Brucciani's, turn right, cross the road, and a little way along is the statue of Eric Morecambe (who used his home town as his stage-name) in 'Bring Me Sunshine' pose, which never fails to attract imitators and photographers.

▶ 217 MARINE ROAD WEST TEL 01524 421386

Rock The Rock Shop has all the traditional seaside rock you could want, plus some with much cheekier and ruder messages than anything anyone who made trips to the Lancashire coast as a child might remember. Then, all you could find was pink rock with Blackpool all the way through, whereas now there's a whole palette of colours and, as for the words, they run all the way from the sentimental to the scandalous.

▶ 272 MARINE ROAD CENTRAL TEL 01524 410434
@ WWW.THE-ROCK-SHOP.CO.UK

The Old Pier Book Shop Just the kind of higgledy-piggledy second-hand bookshop place you want to come across on holiday or during a day out. It has been here since 1994 and is much-loved by both locals and visitors. The lack of obvious organisation means you are forced to browse – that old-fashioned way of turning up books you never knew you wanted or needed to read. Tony Vettese, the owner, runs a Morecambe landmark here, built, it would seem, entirely out of books.

i OPEN 10-6 IN WINTER, AND 10-9ISH IN SUMMER

▶ 287 MARINE ROAD CENTRAL TEL 01524 409360

The Winter Gardens If, as you walk past, you see that this place is open, do go inside to have a look. The exterior is pretty striking but inside it is quite spectacularly theatrical and dramatically shabby. In the summer, there are free concerts and banjoists playing George Formby numbers in one of the most atmospheric interiors you'll ever find. The Winter Gardens opened in 1897 as the Victoria Pavilion, and drew all the big names in music, variety and theatre, from Morecambe and Wise to the Rolling Stones. It closed in 1977 and was bought by the Friends of the Winter Gardens in 2006 who formed a Preservation Trust. So far they have struggled to prevent further depredations to the fabric of the building (Grade II* listed) and to raise enough cash to make serious renovations. All of this means that the theatre now looks fantastically dilapidated, like a film set or the backdrop to a fashion shoot.

The seats have been removed at stalls level, the plaster is crumbling off the curved boxes, the cherubs, and the richly decorated ceiling, and the gilding is tarnished. Yet it remains an immensely evocative place with stained glass panelling and faded gilt lettering. The foyer is brilliant, too, with its mahogany doors, a mosaic floor, and box offices. A very grand staircase with glazed terracotta balustrades and tile dados leads up to the upper levels where the original seats, complete with ashtrays on the backs, remain.

There are occasional events such as ghost hunts and site-specific performances. See the website for details.

▶ 221 MARINE ROAD CENTRAL
@ WWW.THEWINTERGARDENSMORECAMBE.CO.UK

Fish and chips... and mushy peas, curry sauce, a round of white bread and butter, salt and vinegar, and a pot of tea add up to the perfect seaside meal at Atkinson's Fish and Chips.

▶ 16-18 ALBERT ROAD, OFF MARINE DRIVE WEST TEL 01524 410860
@ WWW.FACEBOOK.COM/ATKINSONSFISHANDCHIPS

Morecambe is 30 miles up the M6 from Preston, or you can take the slightly shorter scenic A6 route via Lancaster. By train it takes 35-50 minutes, depending on the time of travel, with one change at Lancaster. The Transpennine Express buses from Preston Bus Station take about an hour.

A town map is available to download at www.morecambe.gov.uk/visitor-map

Carnforth

The station Not so long ago, Carnforth Station was a desolate, wind-swept place with fast, west coast trains whizzing through, and just a few local trains stopping now and again. It had long since lost any of the aura and atmosphere that had been associated with it thanks to its role in an all-time favourite weepy film *Brief Encounter* (1945). The station was the location for the romantic, often heart-breaking, train and plat-form scenes at the fictional Milford Junction, filmed away from London and the threat of enemy bombs, and at night so as not to disrupt railway timetables (all the other scenes were filmed in the south of England and the refreshment room scenes were done in a studio).

Now, though, it's possible to visit the station and dash up the long ramp to the platform like Laura Jesson, desperate to meet Dr Alec Harvey before their trains depart in different directions, and to stand under the very same, huge clock that dictates the timings of this brief love affair. You can even rush into the refreshment room, pretending you have a speck of soot in your eye, in search of a calm, charming doctor to fall in love with.

This is all because Carnforth Station has been rescued and restored with enthusiasm and hard work and is now a Heritage Centre. The handsome 1937 buildings are spruce and clean, and the station rooms between platforms 1 and 2 have been transformed. There is a 1940s style Refreshment Room, based on the one in the film, a 'Brief Encoun-ter' exhibition where, gloriously, you can sit in a cinema seat and watch

the film on a loop, mouthing the dialogue with a cut-glass accent, and a museum about Carnforth and the role of the railways here in the two world wars.

The Refreshment Room is close to the original, complete with polished, hissing tea urn, old stove, proper railway china, and cakes in a glass case (made in the bakery next door, but sadly no Banburys). The only things missing are the exchanges between Albert ("give us a kiss") and Myrtle ("you ought to be ashamed of yourself") and the surging Rachmaninov score. The station master's office with its lovely tiled floor and fireplace is now part of the cafe - this is where Celia Johnson warmed up between takes in the middle of the night. Have a currant slice or something suitably local and a cup of tea, then move to the exhibition, buy a few postcards of film stills, and have a wallow in understated British cinema romance.

i THE REFRESHMENT ROOM OPEN DAILY 9-4

▶ CARNFORTH RAILWAY STATION, WARTON ROAD TEL 01524 732432

@ WWW.REFRESHMENTROOM.COM

i CARNFORTH STATION HERITAGE CENTRE OPEN 10-4 (FREE)

▶ TEL 01524 735165

@ WWW.CARNFORTHSTATION.CO.UK

The town Of course, it's fine to go to Carnforth simply for the *Brief Encounter* connections, to spend a happy hour or so in the station, having tea and a currant slice in the Refreshment Room and watching favourite scenes from the film in the exhibition next door. But if you do have time, it's also worth leaving the station to have a look round the small Lancashire railway town, and perhaps buy a couple of second-hand Penguin paperbacks and a generous wedge of Lancashire cheese to take home.

Carnforth was a small Lancashire village until the mid-nineteenth century when the combination of new iron-smelting works and the arrival of the railways caused it to develop rapidly into a major transport centre. Now, though, it's settling back to being an attractive, small but busy Lancashire market town (market day is Wednesday) with an interesting industrial and railway past which has left its mark in many places, not least in the rows of neat terraced houses built for railway workers.

The station itself has a listed and very unusual signal box which can be seen from the main platform: it is the small but tall, pale stone building which looks like a small Tudor cottage or folly on a raised block. It was built in 1882 and was used until 1903, yet it survives intact and would make a wonderful little office or a lookout tower for train-spotters.

Just across from the station is the Station Hotel (1880) with its lovely, curved stone lettering, a reminder of the days when station hotels were full of 'commercial travellers' and comings and goings. To the left of the station is the old Post Office building (1887) with solidly proud and long-lasting Victorian lettering; there is a still a sorting office behind, sited here so that mail could be easily loaded and unloaded from the trains.

As well as *Brief Encounter* at the station, a further cinematic link can be found, rather surprisingly, in the the Co-Op near the station whose grand, Art Deco/classical white facade dates from 1923; this was once the Kinema and later the Roxy Cinema. It's nice to think of Carnforth audiences coming here to watch the film, and looking in particular for the scenes which were filmed just over the road at the station.

Further up Market Street, past the Co-Op and the war memorial (1924), is the excellent **Carnforth Bookshop** (open Mon-Sat 9-5.30, 38-42 Market Street, www.carnforth books.co.uk) which has been doing good business in new and second-hand books since 1977. It has 100,000 second-hand books in 14 rooms, enough to keep any browser happy. There are seemingly miles of bookshelves here and the vast range of stock is in good order - well laid-out and nicely organised in rooms made comfortable with sofas and chairs and the possibility of tea and coffee.

Not far from the bookshop is a large branch of **Booths** (www.booths. co.uk). If you've never come across Booths, you are in for a supermarket treat. The company was established in 1847, trades only in the North West*, and has never lost sight of its aim to sell the best quality foods sold by 'first-class assistants'. But what makes a Booths supermarket different is that it manages to think small and local on a grand scale, so the large, well-organised shops are full of wonderful produce from nearby farmers and businesses such as damsons from Lyth Valley, Mrs Kirkham's Lancashire cheese, Formby asparagus, Morecambe Bay potted shrimps, and Manx kippers. It also has an outstanding wine range which is always winning awards and putting bigger supermarkets to shame.

Although Carnforth now has the station platform with the most romantic associations in the country, the railway companies' arrival was pre-dated by the canals, and the town is on the Lancaster canal which opened in 1797. There is a canal basin where brightly coloured barges are moored, and there are several good, peaceful canal walks in both directions.

Finally, for enthusiasts of 1930s architecture of which there are many fine examples in nearby Morecambe, there is an austere Art Deco, red-brick cube County Library which was opened in 1937 (Lancaster Road, Morecambe direction).

*In addition to stocking appealing produce, Booths has also managed to appear in many beautiful spots in Lancashire and Cumbria. The Windermere (Lake District) branch is excellent, and there are Booths in Set-tle (start of the spectacular Settle-Carlisle Railway), Knutsford (as part of an Elizabeth Gaskell/*Cranford* visit), Ripon (great cathedral), Ilkley (combine with tea at Bettys), and Lytham (seaside and golf).

Carnforth is 28 miles from Preston, and there are hourly trains between the two; the fastest direct service takes just 25 minutes. A Transpennine Express bus runs from Preston Bus Station to Carnforth Station and takes about an hour (www.tpexpress.co.uk).

Parched Peas recipe

The dried peas can be bought from Matt Wade's greengrocery in the Indoor Market at Preston. Here they are called 'parching peas', but elsewhere the same peas may be labelled 'maple peas', 'grey peas', 'black peas' or 'carlings'. Traditionally eaten around Bonfire Night (with parkin to follow) or at annual fairs, they are deliciously earthy and warming. They are also very easy to make.

SERVES 4

250g parching peas
1 teaspoon bicarbonate of soda
Salt, pepper, malt vinegar

1 Soak the peas overnight in a bowl of water with one teaspoon of bicarbonate of soda.

2 The next day, when you are ready to cook, drain and rinse the peas.

3 Place the peas in a large, non-stick pan and cover with water. Bring to the boil and simmer gently for 40-50 minutes until the peas are cooked and soft, and some have burst open. While cooking, check and stir regularly, adding more water as necessary to prevent the peas drying out. When done, the peas should be in a thick sauce and not be dried out or sitting in runny liquid.

4 Towards the end of cooking, season generously with salt and pepper and stir in.

5 Serve in small white china cups with a good dash of malt vinegar, and eat with a spoon.

PRESTON

Home of the

Parched Pea

Since 1773

Acknowledgements

For their support, encouragement, ideas and help, I would like to thank Nicola Beauman, Sam Brewster, Roz Streeten, Charlotte Berger, Anne Burns-Atkinson, Éireann Lorsung, Lydia Sage, Anna Marie Roos, Jane Graham Maw, Chloe Evans, Catherine Hawley, Ali Dean, and Simon, Tom and Alice Brocket. I would like to say a special thank you to Hilary Machell and Alex Walker at the Harris Museum & Art Gallery. I am particularly grateful to Phoebe Brocket for her assistance and, above all, Sarah Rock who created the book's lovely design.

First published 2015 by Yarnstorm Press
www.yarnstormpress.co.uk

Set in Baskerville and Gotham
Design © Sarah Rock 2015

Printed by Lavenham Press, Suffolk

978-1-910233-02-3

TRAVEL with a BROCKET in your POCKET